TOWARDS A POWERFUL
INNER LIFE

THE JOURNEY OF DEVELOPING
AN INTERNAL SPIRITUALITY,
WHEN OVERWHELMED
BY EXTERNAL CIRCUMSTANCES

GRAHAM COOKE

AN INTERACTIVE JOURNAL

BOOK 6
BEING WITH GOD SERIES

WWW.BRILLIANTBOOKHOUSE.COM

Unless otherwise indicated, all Scripture quotations are taken from The Holy Bible, New King James Version (Copyright © 1979, 1980, 1982 by Thomas Nelson, Inc.) and the New American Standard Bible (Copyright © 1960, 1962, 1963, 1971, 1972, 1973, 1975, 1977, 1995 by The Lockman Foundation).

Please note that Brilliant Book House has made the stylistic choice to capitalize certain words and pronouns that refer to the Father, Son and Holy Spirit, although it may differ from the stylistic choices of other publishers.

Book design by Natalie McGuire Designs, LLC.
Towards a Powerful Inner Life, 1st edition ©2004

BRILLIANT BOOK HOUSE
PO Box 871450
Vancouver, WA, 98687

This book and all other materials published by Graham Cooke are available online at BrilliantBookHouse.com

If you would like more information on Graham Cooke and his ministry, please visit GrahamCooke.com

Brilliant
BOOK HOUSE

ISBN 978-1-934771-00-6

I

DEDICATION

I have been on a compelling spiritual journey since 1972. In the span of years since, my story has involved more friends and companions than I could ever attempt to list here. These are people with whom I have laughed and cried, suffered and persisted alongside. We have received curses against us and had blessings spoken over us. We have all been written off, yet we remain.

We are bigger, stronger, more anointed and still walking with the One who loves us magnificently.

I rejoice because there is still time to add new names to this incredible group of game changers.

TOWARDS A POWERFUL
INNER LIFE

SOUL VERSUS SPIRIT

We are beings at war with ourselves. Inside each of us are two parts in conflict: a soul—otherwise know as the outer man—and a spirit—also know as the inner man. These two pieces of the whole strive for complete control of who you are. Each desperately wants to run the show, but only one can. In Romans 7:14–25, the Apostle Paul wrote about the battle of these two halves, using the word "spiritual" to describe the inner man, and the word "carnal" to describe the outer man:

> For we know that the law is spiritual, but I am carnal, sold under sin. For what I am doing, I do not understand. For what I will to do, that I do not practice; but what I hate, that I do. If, then, I do what I will not to do, I agree with the law that it is good. But now, it is no longer I who do it, but sin that dwells in me. For I know that in me (that is, in my flesh) nothing good dwells; for to will is present with me, but how to perform what is good I do not find. For the good that I will to do, I do not do; but the evil I will not to do, that I practice. Now if I do what I will not to do, it is no longer I who do it, but sin that dwells in me.

> I find then a law, that evil is present with me, the one who wills to do good. For I delight in the law of God according to the inward man. But I see another law in my members, warring against the law of my mind and bringing me

into captivity to the law of sin which is in my members. O wretched man that I am! Who will deliver me from this body of death? I thank God—through Jesus Christ our Lord!

So then, with the mind I myself serve the law of God, but with the flesh the law of sin.

God has called us to be ruled by our spirit, to submit our outer man (our soul) to that inner man. As Paul wrote, we must begin warring against ourselves, subjecting our soul—our mind, emotions, and will—to our spirit—that part of us which connects with God. Before we were Christians, we did what we wanted, we went where we pleased, we ruled our own life. But with salvation came a call from a different king: our soul must bow its knee to the reign of God.

This can be quite a battle. The spirit, which hears the whisper of God, exerts pressure on the soulish will to change its behavior. The soul, conversely, is more in love with the *idea* of God than with God *Himself*. The soul drags its heels, trying desperately to avoid surrendering to the spirit. It manifests itself in willful displays, deluded thinking, and odd emotional behavior. Our soul refuses to surrender easily to our spirit because it wants to be number one. It will rule us to the point of ruining us. For example, the soul believes in self-gratification: it resists God. The spirit, on the other hand, knows the power and satisfaction of God.

Our soul is quite the creation. It does not, because of our finiteness, understand the ways of God. It cannot fathom why He does what He does. Our minds are just too limited by time

> "TO BE TAKEN WITH LOVE FOR A SOUL, GOD DOES NOT LOOK UPON ITS GREATNESS, BUT THE GREATNESS OF ITS HUMILITY."
> -ST. JOHN OF THE CROSS

and space to see the richness of the Lord's activities. When we find ourselves in trouble, our soul knows what it wants from God: "Get me out of here! Lift me up out of this mess!" It tries its best to avoid entering the process of submitting to the spirit.

Souls hate being weak; they would much rather flex their intellectual, willful, or emotional muscles to prove their strength. Our soul does not want to surrender control because it seems illogical to.

Yet soul power must be broken or we cannot serve God effectively. Our soul needs to recognize that it will only be truly happy when we have no authority, but have taken the attitude of serving what God has placed within us: our spirit. The soul will only find peace and fulfillment and full expression when it is a vehicle for our spirit to operate.

Left unconquered, the soul keeps us open and vulnerable to external pressures and attacks. Learning how to live in the spirit gives us the opportunity, because of our devotion and submission to God, to reverse all of the activity of the enemy and render his schemes useless. With the soul in control, the enemy is free to buffet us and leave us in the grip of the very pain we were called to put on him. If we can learn to submit our outer man to our inner man, nothing from the outside world will be able to shake who we are in Christ.

x

The story of sisters Mary and Martha, found in Luke 10:38–42, is a perfect example of one person living under the power of her soul, and one living under the power of her spirit. Mary, whose spirit was drawn and electrified by the spirit of God, sat at Jesus' feet and listened as He spoke and taught. *"Mary has chosen that good part, which will not be taken away from her,"* Jesus said. Martha, on the other hand, had too many preparations on her mind and fell into an emotional outburst to try and get Mary to serve her agenda. *"Martha, Martha, you are worried and troubled about many things,"* Jesus said. *"But one thing is needed."* The issue here is primacy. Martha's concerns were, in fact, legitimate. However, in the context of placing soul under spirit, she had made *doing* more important than *being*. When that happens, we are not living from the inside out, but from the opposite dimension. We must place real value on the presence of God above all other concerns—no matter how pressing.

There are times when we have to work and times when we have to rest; the book of Ecclesiastes makes that clear. We don't always get to sit at the feet of Jesus and do nothing. This story,

> "HOW HAPPY I AM TO SEE MYSELF IMPERFECT AND BE IN NEED OF GOD'S MERCY."
> -ST. THERESE OF THE CHILD JESUS AND THE HOLY FACE

however, is an illustration of what we have given power, when push comes to shove. Does the presence of God have primacy in our life? Have we allowed our spirit to sit at the feet of Jesus? Or are we constantly thinking about our temporal concerns? It seems paradoxical, but if we can learn to rest at Jesus' feet, we will find we can do the temporal things properly.

When we live in our spirit, we don't need reassurance. We have a built-in testimony: the Holy Spirit bears witness with our spirit that we are the children of God.

THE THREE-PART PERSON

According to Scripture, there are three parts to every man and woman who has ever lived: a soul, a spirit, and a body. *"Now may the God of peace Himself sanctify you completely; and may your whole spirit, soul, and body be preserved blameless at the coming of our Lord Jesus Christ,"* Paul wrote in 1 Thessalonians 5:23. Body and soul often conspire and work together against the spirit. In God's design, however, He intended for the Holy Spirit to dwell and mingle with our spirit. That spiritual man would then govern the soul, which is made up of our mind, emotions and will.

To live happily and successfully with God, we must become a vehicle of the spirit. Our body will be used as the outward expression of whatever is in command: our soul or our spirit. To be our fullest expression in Christ, our soul must understand that it cannot, and must not, act on its own volition. The spirit man, according to the relationship it has with the Holy Spirit, must give the soul instruction and authority. The soul has to be won, mastered, and ruled by the spirit if we want to know the higher ways of God. Our soul needs to be saved every day.

The Bible is full of verses explaining the need for the soul to submit to the spirit:

+ *"FOR I DELIGHT IN THE LAW OF GOD ACCORDING TO THE INWARD MAN."* (ROMANS 7:22)

✦ *"...THAT HE WOULD GRANT YOU, ACCORDING TO THE RICHES OF HIS GLORY, TO BE STRENGTHENED WITH MIGHT THROUGH HIS SPIRIT IN THE INNER MAN, THAT CHRIST MAY DWELL IN YOUR HEARTS THROUGH FAITH..."* (EPHESIANS 3:16-17)

✦ *"BUT YOU ARE NOT IN THE FLESH BUT IN THE SPIRIT, IF INDEED THE SPIRIT OF GOD DWELLS IN YOU. NOW IF ANY-ONE DOES NOT HAVE THE SPIRIT OF CHRIST, HE IS NOT HIS."* (ROMANS 8:9)

✦ *"THEREFORE WE DO NOT LOSE HEART. EVEN THOUGH OUR OUTWARD MAN IS PERISHING, YET THE INWARD MAN IS BEING RENEWED DAY BY DAY."* (2 CORINTHIANS 4:16)

When the Bible talks about our innermost being, it is referring to our spirit. When it talks about our outer man, it is referring to our soul and body. God lives in the human spirit; His Holy Spirit mingles with our spirit.

> **"THE INNER MAN, THE SPIRIT, WEARS THE OUTER MAN, THE SOUL AND BODY."**

The concept of inner and outer beings can be likened to clothing. The inner man, the spirit, wears the outer man, the soul and body. To be effective for Christ, we must release the inner man. To be fulfilled and joyful, the spirit must govern the soul.

WHAT IS THE SPIRIT?

Our spirit is only ever subject to, and in the presence of God. It is the part of us which is eternal. It constantly communes with God Himself, only having dealings with Him. To interact with the physical world, it must operate through your soul and body. The spirit is the part of us that finds its refuge in God. When the writer of Psalm 91 sang *"He is my refuge and my fortress; My God, in Him I will trust,"* he was referring to his spirit finding safety within God's presence. It is a place inside of us that cannot be touched by anything out in the world because it lives in the presence of God.

The Father has several, wonderfully visual images of what life in the spirit looks like. He is our refuge, fortress, high tower, and hiding place; we nestle under the shadow of His wings. One of the prime goals of our relationship with God must be to learn to access these safe places daily. We need to learn the business of stepping back into the internal provision of God in the spirit. Do we take refuge in Him when under pressure and attack? Do we wait patiently to discern His heart before committing ourselves to an action? This is the loving discipline of the spirit which takes the control away from our soul so that we can respond to God and not react to events.

When the enemy comes calling, we shouldn't rush out to meet him in battle. Instead, we should retreat into our spirit man first, entering the presence of God. When we're there, God can give us intelligence, resources, and strategy to destroy the enemy. In leadership, the first difficulties we face are not the work of the ministry or other people, it's with ourselves. We are our own worst enemy, by refusing to subject our soul to our spirit. If we allow our spirit to govern the way we act and lead, we will have God's empowerment to carry on.

WEAKNESS OF THE SOUL

Our soul is not our enemy. If we have committed our lives to Jesus, it loves God. It is, unfortunately, like a pimply adolescent that lives in our skin. Our soul wants to meet God on our own terms. "I want God to do things for me, but I want to run my own life," it moans. "I want to live how I like to live." Our soul wants to relegate God to a basic insurance policy: if I need a bit of help, He's there. Otherwise, He's locked away in the safety deposit box.

The soul was designed to serve, a statement which begs the question: "If it's not serving God, who is it serving?" Our soul will serve us, and even the enemy. It fights to stay in control. Religious activity provides a set of external rules that our soul strives to keep so it can maintain control of its destiny. Much of the pharisaical activity recorded in Scripture was soulish and controlling, concerned more with retaining power than demonstrating servanthood; more aware of status than humility; and more open to leading with power than fathering and mentoring. We are all Pharisees, being healed.

> "IT IS SWEET TO THINK OF JESUS; BUT IT IS SWEETER TO DO HIS WILL."
> -BLESSED MARY OF JESUS CRUCIFIED

Up until the time of salvation, our soul ruled unopposed through our mind, will, and emotions. Our spirit was dead, with no concept of God. Before salvation, we lived as we pleased. We were dominated by soulishness and self-interest (see Figure 1).

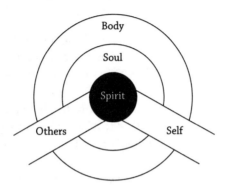

FIGURE 1

God breaks into our lives at salvation, causing a massive battle within ourselves. The spirit is boosted, and begins to push the soul to express love for God, ourselves, and other people. The soul hates this, for it is no longer in full control. We are born again, and our spirit is revitalized. The soul must submit to that spirit man, or it will suffer one of two fates: it either becomes carnal or flesh.

When we are born again, our spirit is revitalized (see Figure 2). Now the battle for supremacy begins. We come under the conflict of two natures, as detailed in Romans 7:14–25. Salvation brings another measure of rule to our lives. Soul power has to be broken or we cannot serve God effectively.

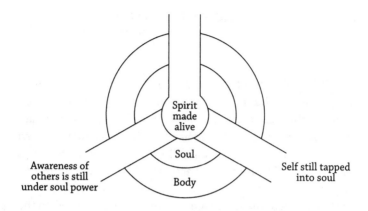

FIGURE 2

Flesh is the sinful appetite of the *body*, anything we do for self-gratification: sex, drugs, overeating, anything. *Carnality* is the sinful appetite of the *soul*, or what happens when we run our lives through the soul, and not the spirit. Carnality is about us wanting to live for God, but refusing to relinquish control to Him on how that looks. We become religious and pharisaical, living to please ourselves but calling it godliness.

AN ANCIENT CONFLICT

This epic battle of soul versus spirit is not a recent development. Modern humanity is in good company with every generation who has walked the Earth since the beginning of man. When Adam and Eve ate the bad fruit in the Garden of Eden, they were immediately changed. Their souls became the rulers of their lives. The couple had access to God's wisdom through the spirit, but the enemy convinced them there was more than that available to them. The temptation in Eden centered on the issue of wisdom, as we can read in Genesis 3:1–5:

Now the serpent was more cunning than any beast of the field which the LORD God had made. And he said to the woman, "Has God indeed said, 'You shall not eat of every tree of the garden'?"

And the woman said to the serpent, "We may eat of the fruit of the trees of the garden; but of the fruit of the tree which is in the midst of the garden, God has said, 'You shall not eat it, nor shall you touch it, lest you die.'"

Then the serpent said to the woman, "You will not surely die. For God knows that in the day you eat of it your eyes will be opened, and you will be like God, knowing good and evil."

Satan's advice to man was to reach across the boundaries set by God and seize the resources of wisdom for himself.

"You will be like God," he said. The serpent conned man into believing that there could be a life without dependence on God. "Depend on yourself," he essentially lied, "and when you get into a really sticky situation, then call on God. In the meantime, go with what your soul tells you." This is a lie that every man and woman has struggled with since.

Israel's history is littered with examples of when the nation turned its collective back on God and found itself in terrible situations. *"Everyone did what was right in his own eyes,"* as the book of Judges put it many times. In those moments of rebellion, a famine or invading kingdom would strike; the Israelites, in fear and disarray, would repent and beg God to save them. In His mercy, the Lord would heal the situation, delivering the unfaithful nation. For a while, Israel would again serve Him until drifting back into its old pattern of doing what seemed right to their own minds, emotions and wills.

Satan lied, of course. There was no wisdom in the tree of good and evil. In fact, God's wisdom was contained in the tree of life. The tree of good and evil brought death, and man was driven out of the Garden of Eden. A redeemer now had to be raised up to come and open the door for man to return. In the meantime, fallen men and women strove to live by their own wisdom, motivated by selfish ambition and jealousy.

We see this pattern especially clearly in the field of philosophy. What is philosophy but man's wisdom? It's mostly about how some man thinks about something. I often visit the philosophical section when I am in a bookstore to find out what man is thinking about now. If you let your spirit do the looking through those books and thoughts, you'll come to a startling realization: rarely does philosophy take us into the presence of God and make us conscious of Him. Rather, it appeals to our mind, helping us explain something of our state of being, but adding nothing to our standing in Christ. It can give credence to our soul but may contribute nothing to our spirit. It is empty and potentially deceptive, like a cloud without rain.

Philosophy sounds great but it doesn't actually mean anything. It doesn't connect with our spirit, it just makes us more self-absorbed. Intellectual people often struggle with a similar issue: they live so much in their minds that they have no spiritual perception whatsoever. When you talk to someone whose intellect is their god, they will try and defeat you with logic and science.

> "YOU WANT TO HAVE A SPIRITUAL CONVERSATION, BUT THEY WANT TO HAVE A SOULISH ONE."

It's frustrating: you want to have a spiritual conversation, but they want to have a soulish one.

Philosophy is but one example of how man devises means to attain his own goals, falling prey to a wisdom that is earthly, unspiritual, and ultimately demonic, as James 3:15–18 tells us:

> *This wisdom does not descend from above, but is earthly, sensual, demonic. For where envy and self-seeking exist, confusion and every evil thing are there. But the wisdom that is from above is first pure, then peaceable, gentle, willing to yield, full of mercy and good fruits, without partiality and without hypocrisy. Now the fruit of righteousness is sown in peace by those who make peace.*

When we hear wisdom, we feel good about ourselves. It touches our hearts and helps us to see God in a better light. That fresh light gives us a better view of ourselves as well. It touches how we feel about who we are. Yet when man ate the fruit from the tree of good and evil, the spirit was dethroned. Divine order in fallen humanity was lost. Our spirits were cut off from God, and we lost our God-given authority and power. Man became more aware of his own nakedness, what he was not and did not possess, than the provision and covering of the Father's love. God's love clothed us in righteousness but, now man sought to cover himself at the expense of his relationship with the Father.

Adam and Eve, and all of their descendants, now had to fill that void of power and authority in their lives. The soul swelled up and took the lead. Our soul's power—what makes our mind, will and emotions happy—and our physical appetites became the driving force behind our lives.

THE DISCIPLES' BATTLE

Another example of the battle of soul versus spirit can be found in the lives of Jesus' disciples in Mark 4. Jesus, the greatest weatherman of all time, saw a storm brewing on the Sea of Galilee and made a suggestion: "Let's go for a boat ride." He and

His disciples piled into the boat and set sail. A few minutes later, Jesus was asleep in the back.

Many of Jesus' friends were experienced fishermen but they had never met a storm like this—a storm engineered by God for a particular purpose. Things were bad, the waves were fierce, and Jesus was asleep. How could He have been so tranquil? How could He have slept through this? What was wrong with Him?

I have seen many times that when you put a man living in his spirit, in a room with a man living in his soul, and subject them to the same experience, the soulish man will accuse the spiritual man of not caring. Why? Because he is peaceful. How could he care if he's not showing anxiety? We have made a virtue out of being anxious. Actually, the spiritual man does care, but he is caring from a different place. The soulish man wears his worry in his mind, emotions and will; the spiritual man wears his in the presence of God. Anxiety will never overcome anything.

> "PEACE, BE STILL."
> – JESUS, MARK 4:39

When we learn to live in the realm of the spirit, people think we don't care about things. *"Teacher, do you not care that we are perishing?"* the disciples asked Jesus in Mark 4:38. Of course He did. He just stood up and did the thing they should have done: spoke to what was happening in the physical world from what was happening in His spirit.

THE CANCER OF THE SOUL

Our soul will be a hindrance if we do not bring it under the rule and authority of our spirit. I became a Christian on my nineteenth birthday. For nineteen years, my spirit was dead to God. My human spirit was alive and functioning but was *"dead in trespasses and sins"* (Ephesians 2:1). The spirit of unregenerate people has not ceased to exist.

Life and death in the Scriptures always centers on relationship. Life means to be rightly related to God who is the source of all life. Death means being cut off from God through sin.

The human spirit in its unregenerate state is still able to connect with the spiritual realm but can only reach and touch the dark side where death reigns. This is the realm of evil within the occult, which may appear benign and attractive but contains evil and seductive spirits that can suck us into a realm that is demonic and terrifying. For this reason the Scriptures totally prohibit spiritualism, divination and fortune telling, as it leads vulnerable people into potential and actual enslavement.

My soul and my body governed every aspect of my life—I did whatever pleased me. Then one day, the light of God shone into me. Everything changed! From that moment on, I have been at odds with myself, working to make my soul submit to my spirit. Before salvation, the spirit is dead, unconnected to God. When Jesus came in, He changed all of that, plugging my spirit into His. I was truly alive.

I used to make my own decisions, reigning and ruling through my soul. My mind, emotions, and will dominated through my body. I was self-centered, self-referential, and cold, offering only conditional love. "What can I get out of this relationship?" I thought. "What's in it for me?" When I lived in my body and soul, I was always subject to external influences.

Before we are saved, we are buffeted by the enemy in so many ways. Some soulish men and women understand the will in an occult way, using it to dominate other people and lead them away from God. They use systems and philosophies like New Age to take people on a quest far from the Lord. All the will wants is power over other people. Most who go into witchcraft and the occult are in it for pride, power, money, and sex. They want to dominate other people. Witchcraft is a suffocating force which is why we must get rid of it in the Church.

Other people are at the mercy of their emotions. Everything is about feelings, "I'm feeling this," they say. A lot of counseling has too much to do with emotions, which makes what we're feeling at any given moment the central thing in our lives. I agree with what the Eagles sang: "I'd like to find your inner child and kick its little backside." We're told to release our inner self, and that our emotions and what we feel is all-important.

> "IT IS NOT SO ESSENTIAL TO THINK MUCH AS TO LOVE MUCH."
> –ST. TERESA OF JESUS

Others are dominated by bodily appetites and physical drives. It could be sex, it could be food, it could be fitness. We go into a gym and find ourselves surrounded by body Nazis: all looking at our puny shapes and shaking their heads in disdain. They are there, hours and hours, day after day. Some people are absolutely dominated by how they look. They have to have an extra room to hold all of their clothes. Other people are held by images and material possessions.

There is nothing wrong with looking good, or owning something, unless it dominates our life. We can be well-dressed, own a beautiful house, and drive a nice car, but we cannot be dominated by those things. The result of serving these other items is ruinous. Our soul and body were not meant to rule us. They are incapable of guiding us. All that happens is a power struggle between all of our competing desires, all clamoring to be satisfied, all claiming to be of paramount importance.

The result is that we end up hopelessly at war with ourselves—divided, imbalanced, and a slave to sin. We see this phenomenon in the Corinthian church. These people had become Christians but did not understand that the spirit needed to rule the soul. Paul, as an apostle, had to correct their carnality. He identified their sexual sin, which was horrific: one churchgoer is even having sex with his mother (1 Corinthians 5:1). Their souls ran the show in Corinth, and Paul had to step in and right the ship.

"For I indeed, as absent in body but present in spirit, have already judged (as though I were present) him who has so done this deed. In the name of our Lord Jesus Christ, when you are gathered together, along with my spirit, with the power of our Lord Jesus Christ, deliver such a one to Satan for the destruction of the flesh,

that his spirit may be saved in the day of the Lord Jesus," Paul wrote in 1 Corinthians 5:3-5.

Paul knew, in his spirit, what was happening in Corinth, and, as an apostle, brought correction. His desire was to protect the spiritual men and women of Corinth from soulish self-gratification.

THE UNREGENERATE MAN

It is absolutely essential that we understand what we have been called out of. The unregenerate person, one who lives according to their soul, not their spirit, is wide open to the power of the demonic. Our spirit, while dead to the things of God, was alive to the touch of the enemy. When a person becomes involved in occult things, evil power can be transferred into their spirit. As a result, the spirit has lost its link with God, the source of life, and has become no better than the rest of man's fallen nature.

Man's spirit is created to connect to an external source of power or authority. Therefore, the unregenerate man's spirit has fallen under the power of satan and is dead to God, as Paul wrote in Ephesians 2:1–3:

And you He made alive, who were dead in trespasses and sins, in which you once walked according to the course of this world, according to the prince of the power of the air, the spirit who now works in the sons of disobedience, among whom also we all once conducted ourselves in the lusts of our flesh, fulfilling the desires of the flesh and of the mind, and were by nature children of wrath, just as the others.

Paul was writing about a spirit under the power of evil. If you travel to minister in certain parts of the world, you cannot simply go in and preach the gospel. First, you must do signs and wonders to deliver people of evil spirits. They have to be set free to hear the Good News. Only then can they be saved.

I have experienced this in my own ministry throughout the third world, where a Christian has to go head-to-head with a witch doctor or someone else. Ministry in those places is about continual confrontation with the powers of darkness. The battle is often physical and quite natural. The demonic is visible and intimidating. Natural laws are overturned by those in occult ministry; spiritual confrontations have to be played out on a natural level.

Living in the spirit is essential or one cannot compete with the works of darkness. To be successful in sharing the gospel, you must know exactly who you are and what you have to overcome. These people's spirits, so choked by the demonic, only understand power. Your word means nothing out there. What they want to know is, "Is your God stronger than mine?" And if He is, they will follow Him.

In the west, the demonic force is much more subtle, rooted in unreality and fantasy. It manifests itself in the lemming-like headlong pursuit of relentless self-gratification. Millions of people are financially in debt in the chase for self-worth and the feel-good factor. Emotional healing is big business in the west. Mental illness is a modern-day plague with suicides amongst all generations at an all-time high. It is the spirit of the age, and the western church, in particular, is influenced by it. Soulish Christianity is rampant in the west in a church driven almost universally by consumerism. "My needs, my rights, my desires," dominate the thinking of western believers who pick and choose the church program most able to fulfill their requirements. There is little thought of service, sacrifice, or meeting the needs of others. It's little wonder that the occult religions have taken hold in the west. It is easy to outwit a complacent church. Soulish Christianity is a pushover for the forces of darkness. The enemy wins every battle with ease because most Christians fail to show up for the fight.

We must ask ourselves some important questions:

- WHEN WAS THE LAST TIME I SUCCESSFULLY ENCOUNTERED THE ENEMY?

- HOW MANY TIMES HAVE I GONE THROUGH DIFFICULT CIRCUMSTANCES AND FAILED TO NOTICE THE POWER BEHIND THE SITUATION?

- WHEN WAS THE LAST TIME I TOOK SPECIFIC THOUGHTS CAPTIVE OR CONTROLLED MY EMOTIONS BY FAITH?

Now reflect on these issues. Is the inability to rule in our own lives directly linked to our ineffectiveness in spiritual warfare? In John 14:30 Jesus said, *"The ruler of this world is coming, and he has nothing in Me."* Paul expressed it this way in Ephesians 4:27—*"[Give no] place to the devil."*

us to be like that with Him. Be ready for every new day.
His grace that is new every morning. Today, together,
going to whip the world. And if we don't, there's always
row.

od develops our faith to rule over our feelings. Faith is
looded, and has no emotion attached to it. We can believe
thing even if we don't feel it. Many of us have become
ers to our emotions, allowing them to run the show. God
to put that back into its proper order. Feelings are like
il end of a dog, they will just go along with whatever is in
ol. Emotions, in God's order, serve us and aid us in being
Him, people, and ourselves.

od uses His unconditional love to kill religiosity. The reli-
part of us has to be shocked by the nature of God. How
He love somebody that much? Does God love Saddam Hus-
as much as He loves you? Does He love Osama bin Laden
uch as He loves you? Absolutely. God loves those men.
they're monsters!" our religiosity objects. Still, God loves
n. I'm not defending them or their actions, but God does
them. His love is shocking in that regard.

A true spirituality is being cultivated by God, not a soul-
one. We see the difference very visibly in how we pray.
en your soul prays for strength, it always has itself as the
is: "Father, I pray that You will strengthen me by Your spirit,
bling me to stand and overcome my weakness so that I can
t and break through circumstances." That prayer is packed
of references to ourselves. The soul wants to receive power
t can do something.

Christians are never weak numerically. One person, with God, is always in the majority. But we are weak when we don't

> **"ONE PERSON, WITH GOD, IS ALWAYS IN THE MAJORITY."**

understand who we are in God or what He has provided for us. That's why the Church is so atrophied in many parts of the world. People die spiritually every day of the week trying to reach the lost in these occult-laced places. There is a demonic power out there that is very, very real—which is why it is vital for us to get God's power flowing in our lives.

Unregenerate men and women can contact the spiritual realm; their spirits are functional, but dead to God. If a spirit cannot connect with God, it will connect with something—any-thing—else. If it will not reach for the third Heaven, where God dwells, it will settle for contact with the second Heaven, home of satan and his demons.

I've met occult people who move in genuine power; they can prophesy incredibly accurately. This is nothing new; Acts 16 could have told us that. A slave girl, possessed by a spirit of divination, had followed Paul and Silas around for days, proph-esying: *"These men are the servants of the Most High God, who proclaim to us the way of salvation."* That prophetic word is com-pletely accurate. It's more than that, it's almost worshipful: "The Most High God," she said. Yet her words were not from the Spirit of God. Scripture tells us that Paul was grieved in his spirit by the girl's plight, so he turned to her and said to the demon, *"I command you in the name of Jesus Christ to come out of her,"* and it did.

> "I SURRENDERED UNTO HIM ALL THERE WAS OF ME, EVERYTHING! THEN FOR THE FIRST TIME, I REALIZED WHAT IT MEANT TO HAVE REAL POWER."
> -KATHRYN KUHLMAN

Humanity, in its unregenerate state, can have a relationship with spiritual beings that are not of God. Their spirits have reached out for something because it must connect with an external source. Human spirits will reach into the realm of death and darkness for that connection, which explains the proliferation of spiritism, New Age, occultism, tarot cards, and pagan religions. These are all death.

"There is a way that seems right to a man, but its end is the way of death," Solomon wrote in Proverbs 14:12. Behind all of these activities is a demonic presence looking to suck the human spirit dry.

SPIRIT LIFE

A spirit in relationship with God experiences such abundant life that it is almost difficult to describe. When our spirit has submitted to God, and begun to take control of our soul, amazing fruit is produced. We love others more, because we ourselves are fully immersed and settled in God's love.

We have been made in the image and likeness of God. Our spirits were intended by Him to relate us with God, enabling us to receive wisdom and life from Him. Relationship with God

is what the Bible calls life. So to be rig[...] life, and to be cut off from Him is dea[...] ing, crying, and working, but we are s[...] we have no communion with God, the [...]

We are always welcome in God's pr[...] like a much-loved child. It's our job to lov[...] is alive, our minds can have life and p[...] our spirit and into our mortal body. As [...] 5:17, *"For if by the one man's offense death r[...] much more those who receive abundance [...] of righteousness will reign in life through [...] the One, Jesus Christ."* The pathway to [...] a glorious life is determined by how we [...] set ourselves before God.

We can come boldly into God's [...] presence when we are alive in the spirit. [...] When my wife, Heather, was pregnant [...] with our second child, God told me that [...] boy and that he would make me laugh all [...] "He's going to make you smile, Grae," God [...] teach you to be a son before Me."

God was right: Seth was a character fr[...] ning. Halfway out during the delivery Seth [...] I laughed: it was as if he was introducing hi[...] ready, folks!" He has been exactly what God [...] tined to be. I have learned so much of how t[...] father by watching Seth. He is exuberant, rea[...] "Tomorrow is another day!" Seth's life makes [...]

When a spirit-led man or woman prays, it asks God to do whatever He wants to do: "Father, thank You, that in my weakness, You are strength. I submit to Your rule. Come and be my strength—live in me, and overcome me with Your power. Inhabit these circumstances and glorify Your name in all You achieve." This prayer is completely different from the first one.

> "WE HAD A MIGHTY DOWNPOURING OF THE HOLY SPIRIT LAST SATURDAY NIGHT. THIS WAS PRECEDED BY THE CORRECTING OF THE PEOPLE'S VIEW OF TRUE WORSHIP: NUMBER ONE, TO GIVE UNTO GOD, NOT TO RECEIVE. NUMBER TWO, TO PLEASE GOD, NOT TO PLEASE OURSELVES."
> -EVAN ROBERTS

God is breaking our self-preoccupation. Me, me, me: that season is ending. He is making us considerate, open-hearted, and generous through the work of His Cross. We must enjoy our weakness, because it is through that weakness which God flows.

The Holy Spirit has an agenda for us. He wants us to come under His influence as He reveals and forms Christ in us. Jesus and the Holy Spirit are conspiring together for the glory of God.

"If then you were raised with Christ, seek those things which are above, where Christ is, sitting at the right hand of God. Set your mind on things above, not on things on the earth. For you died, and your life is hidden with Christ in God," Paul wrote in Colossians 3:1–3. Our goal is to seek the things which are above both us and the enemy.

There are three levels of spirituality that we need to understand. The first level, what some call the first Heaven, is the natural realm in which we live all the time. The second level, what some call the second Heaven, is the realm where the demonic resides. The third and highest level, what some call the third Heaven, is where God lives. *"But God, who is rich in mercy, because of His great love with which He loved us, even when we were dead in trespasses, made us alive together with Christ (by grace you have been saved), and raised us up together, and made us sit together in the heavenly places in Christ Jesus,"* Paul wrote in Ephesians 2:4–6.

> "WE GET A PERSPECTIVE OF GOD IN THE THIRD LEVEL THAT WE CANNOT GET WHEN WE ARE ON THE GROUND."

The second level is where we do battle with the enemy, but the third level is where we are supposed to be living. The tragedy for most Christians is that they are earthbound—stuck on the first level—in their spirituality. They are so dominated by fear, logic, and reason that they can only look for physical evidence. But when we look for the evidence of God, we go above the first and second levels, above the principalities and powers, and dwell with Him.

Our goal must be to seek things which are not just above us, but above the enemy. Search out the third Heaven, where God lives. We get a perspective of God in the third level that we cannot get when we are on the ground. It's the difference between being an eagle and a turkey. We must set our mind on Christ above, not on the things of the Earth.

The key is to hide our lives with Christ in God. A spirit-led life is wrapped up in Jesus, and protected by that refuge. If you are in Christ, He guards you. In the face of difficulty, we must step back into our spirit man and let Jesus protect us.

Otherwise, the soul will try to do it for us, and that initiative is doomed to failure.

When we are attacked, we must not react. Instead, we should respond to God. Don't look at the circumstances, look at God . Step back into the spirit. Sometimes, the best thing to do is say nothing. Let people unload on you; then, ignore the temptation to lash back, and instead step into your spirit and the comfort of Christ. If you try to give out like for like, you're going to get hurt; but if you step back into your spirit, you're going to get healed.

God wants to bring us into a higher level of spirituality. Our spirit and His Spirit will mingle as we set our minds on the things above—having our soul submit to our spirit. God is intentional about everything in our life. Knowing that, we can go into every situation and know that it is about our soul submitting to His will, as communicated to our spirit. In conflict, our prayers should be simple:

- LORD, I WANT TO GIVE IN TO YOU RIGHT NOW.
- LORD, I QUIT. PLEASE TAKE OVER.
- LORD, TEACH ME YOUR WAYS.
- LORD, SHOW ME YOUR PATH.
- LORD, SHOW ME WHAT TO DO.

If you don't get any indication from God, don't do anything! It's better for us to be killed than for us to kill someone else. If we get killed, we can be easily resurrected. If we spiritually murder someone, we're trapped: not only will we have to apologize to God, but we will have to go and apologize to the other person as well.

BROKENNESS IS THE KEY

The process of bringing the soul under the governance of the spirit is called brokenness. This breaking from within is accomplished by the work of the Cross. For nineteen years, I did things my way. God, however, had a different plan for my life, and worked to break my strength. God doesn't come to give us strength, He comes to break it and lead our soul into weakness. *"So the last will be first, and the first last. For many are called, but few chosen,"* Jesus said in Matthew 20:16. When our soul has been wrestled to the floor, our spirit man can step up and be seen. God wants to break our power, and deliver us into a place where our weakness is welcomed.

In brokenness, what commonly occurs first is our dependence upon the nature of God. Our relationship becomes one of worship, thanksgiving and acceptance of His right to rule.

Secondly, our heart changes towards others (see Figure 3) and our attitude and approach to people begin to be adjusted. We start learning to love other people.

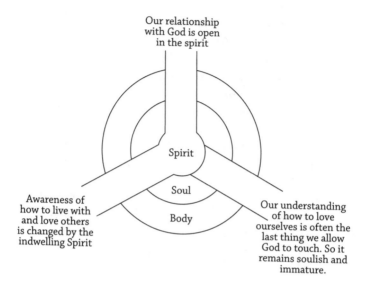

Our relationship with God is open in the spirit

Spirit

Soul

Body

Awareness of how to live with and love others is changed by the indwelling Spirit

Our understanding of how to love ourselves is often the last thing we allow God to touch. So it remains soulish and immature.

FIGURE 3

Typically, this is very difficult and takes quite an internal battle. Unless our attitude toward ourselves is radically changed (this is normally the last area to be adjusted), then our love is often conditional and based on another's performance. Where there is no self love, our love for others is limited.

Three times in his epistles, Paul prayed and asked God to remove a "thorn" in his flesh. He had at least three seasons of begging God to take it away from him. He needed these three seasons, because he refused to hear God saying "no" the first two. God wanted Paul to understand that His strength is made perfect in his servant's weakness. Finally, Paul understood the lesson, as we read in 2 Corinthians 12:7–10:

> And lest I should be exalted above measure by the abundance of the revelations, a thorn in the flesh was given to me, a messenger of Satan to buffet me, lest I be exalted above measure. Concerning this thing I pleaded with the Lord three times that it might depart from me. And He said to me, "My grace is sufficient for you, for My strength is made perfect in weakness." Therefore most gladly I will rather boast in my infirmities, that the power of Christ may rest upon me. Therefore I take pleasure in infirmities, in reproaches, in needs, in persecutions, in distresses, for Christ's sake. For when I am weak, then I am strong.

> "THE GUIDANCE OF THE SPIRIT IS GENERALLY BY GENTLE SUGGESTIONS OR DRAWINGS, AND NOT IN VIOLENT PUSHES; AND IT REQUIRES GREAT CHILDLIKENESS OF HEART TO BE FAITHFUL TO IT. THE SECRET OF BEING MADE WILLING LIES IN A DEFINITE GIVING UP OF OUR WILL. AS SOON AS WE PUT OUR WILL ON TO GOD'S SIDE, HE IMMEDIATELY TAKES POSSESSION OF IT AND BEGINS TO WORK IN US TO WILL AND TO DO OF HIS GOOD PLEASURE."
> -HANNAH WHITALL SMITH

When we learn to enjoy our weakness, an expectancy that God is going to work on our behalf is birthed. Usually the first thing God seeks to break in the lives of Christians is our attitudes toward other people. The Holy Spirit rushes in and we start thinking about other people. He touches our souls, begins to change our hearts, and we discover how to truly love others. A soul touched by God loves Him, and is drawn to Him in relationship. That shift prompts the same soul to love others.

It is possible to be touched by God but not changed—Samson and Solomon are two examples of this point. Samson's life was anointed by God, but his lifestyle was just one indiscretion after another. He was raised up to be a champion of a nation, delivering Israel freedom from her enemies. Instead, he wound up as a bald, blind, and bound prisoner of the very people he was called to defeat. He was a laughingstock. Samson's only recourse was to pull down an entire building, killing himself and as many enemies as he could. Was this the plan of God for Samson? I don't think so; I think God had a grander purpose for his life, but Samson's soulishness led him into disaster.

Solomon had a tremendous relationship with God. "Ask me for anything you want, and I'll give it to you," God said to him in a dream. Solomon asked for wisdom, and the Lord gave him that and everything else he could have ever dreamed of. Solomon fulfilled his father's dream and built a temple for God. Can you imagine what it must have been like on the day the temple was dedicated? The presence of God was so thick that it must have been impossible to stand. A nation did some carpet time!

With all of this communication with God, how could Solomon have ended up so bitter, so distracted by his lust? He was a king who started so brightly but finished poorly. He was touched, but not changed, by God because he refused to allow his soul's power to be broken.

A soul in charge of its own spirituality often becomes religious and pharisaical. It creates hundreds of rules for people, all meant to keep everything under control. The soul will manipulate everything it can to keep its reign intact. It uses people, but does not release them. A soulish relationship is conditional, based on appearances and what a person can deliver.

Brokenness occurs gradually. We wish we could get it all done in a single weekend, moving from soulishness to spirit-led life in three easy steps. It doesn't work that way; it's a process. We have to learn powerlessness in order to receive power. We have to learn weakness and helplessness in order to gain authority.

When God breaks us, He breaks us wide open. In that shattered mirror, we see who we are supposed to be. The soul, which has been hiding that true life from us, is broken and out of the way. At that moment, there is a lightening of the spirit that happens—for the first time, we see who God has called us to be. It is an incredible

> "WE HAVE TO LEARN POWERLESSNESS IN ORDER TO RECEIVE POWER. WE HAVE TO LEARN WEAKNESS AND HELPLESSNESS IN ORDER TO GAIN AUTHORITY."

moment, and makes all of the pain, rejection, humiliation, and betrayal we have faced completely worthwhile.

When Joseph's brothers sold the young dreamer into slavery, he had a choice: he could have carried on his life twisted and hateful, or he could choose to be healed of that rejection. He chose to let his spirit guide his life. When his brothers, years later, stood before him, desperate and penitent, Joseph absolved them of all responsibility: *"But now, do not therefore be grieved or angry with yourselves because you sold me here; for God sent me before you to preserve life,"* Joseph said in Genesis 45:5. Joseph's soul was broken before the Lord, and he was able to see what God was telling his spirit.

In Genesis 32, Jacob had to wrestle with an angel to have something broken and come under the rule of God. The angel wrenched his hip out of its socket, leaving Jacob to limp the rest of his life as a physical manifestation of a spiritual brokenness.

We must understand that God has to break our capacity to self-rule. The true word of the cross is this: *"Nevertheless not My will, but Yours, be done,"* as Jesus prayed in Luke 22:42. The only form of control that is acceptable in the church is self-control. A great church leadership team should bring its parishioners to a

> "A GREAT CHURCH LEADERSHIP TEAM SHOULD BRING ITS PARISHIONERS TO A PLACE WHERE WE GOVERN OUR OWN LIVES."

place where we govern our own lives. If we have to be governed by our church leadership, there is something wrong with us. The role of leaders is to serve the purpose of God in the company that we are part of, and to facilitate people to come into a deeper relationship with God so they can govern themselves.

A self-governed person who chooses to submit their soul to their spirit doesn't have to talk about commitment. We're doing it, being it, enjoying it. We must open our lives to the spirit, seeing the fruit of the Holy Spirit, especially self-control, ripen.

What is God breaking? He is breaking our dominating, manipulative self. He is breaking the tendency to use our intelligence to intimidate people. He is breaking the desire to use physical size to domineer. He is breaking this, in all of its forms and subtlety. He is breaking the way some people can destroy a room with a look. He is breaking anything that isn't of the spirit.

God is calling us to learn to become humble and submissive to Him. He is calling us, once it has been submitted to the spirit, to put our soul in proper order: will first, which affects our mind, and touches our emotions. A soulish man always puts his will last; a spiritual man puts his will first in the order of the soul—reasserting his will as a vehicle of the spirit. The will enables us to develop our minds into the mind of Christ. Having the mind of Christ is where we constantly give our thinking over to God, instinctively and intuitively thinking of something the same way God thinks of it. We can see life from God's perspective.

"SATAN TREMBLES WHEN HE SEES THE WEAKEST SAINT UPON HIS KNEES."
-WILLIAM COWPER

We are all children of God, but it is our capacity for suffering that leads us into the path of experiencing His glory through sonship. We are all children, all heirs of God. But if we do not win the battle of spirit over soul, we will never inherit the fullness of God. Like Israel in their first trip around the desert, we will only be able to see glimpses of the Promised Land until we bow our knee to God's authority.

LOVE YOURSELF AND OTHERS

||||||||||||||||||||||||||||||||||||||||||||||||||||||||||||||||||||||||||||||||||||||||||||||||||||||||||||||||||||||||||||||

Brokenness feels very risky to pursue, but it is the only way to a truly blessed life. Until our true self is released to be loved and accepted, it will protect itself from harm. The best form of protection is usually to attack someone else. Knock them down a peg to lift yourself up. Most of us have built a defensive perimeter through our life's experiences. This is what psychologists call "learned behavior." We don't trust other people, which usually translates into a mistrust of God.

Self-acceptance is the key to loving others. It is vital that we have the right opinion of ourselves. To do that, we need to know what God has saved us from and the work He still wants to do in our lives. We must be realistic in our assessments of our lives: "I am where I am in God, and I like being there. I know God has more to change, but by His grace I'm going to make it." I love the fact that I love where I am with God right now. I know what He wants to change next and I am doing my best to cooperate.

Until "self" is released to be loved and accepted, it will protect itself from harm. Our true self, wrapped up in the spirit and living in the love and pleasure of God, is completely unafraid of being hurt. *"There is no fear in love; but perfect love casts out fear, because fear involves torment. But he who fears has not been made perfect in love. We love Him because He first loved us,"* says 1 John 4:18–19. Figure 4 illustrates this aspect of brokenness.

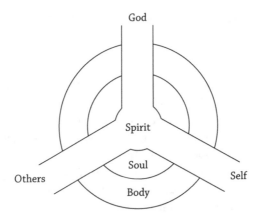

FIGURE 4

Most of the teaching on love in the church centers on loving God or other people. Very little of it talks about loving ourselves. We have been taught how to subjugate ourselves, but not how to love ourselves without being selfish. Loving ourselves out of our soul is selfish; loving ourselves because of what God has done in our spirit is beautiful. We have never learned that distinction.

If the Spirit of Christ does not rule over our soul, we will always require reassurance about our relationship with God. "I don't know if God loves me," we will moan. "I think He's angry with me. He's fed up with me. I've screwed up so many times; I'll never be anything for Him."

We must hear God when He tells us that He likes us. As we mature in Him, we will hear that more and more, in different ways. "I like you," He says. "I love you 100 percent." Whenever we respond to His touch, changing our ways to be more like His, He'll like us again. It never wavers. He has plans to change us, but He is happy with where we are.

In relationships with others, human nature is to withhold part of ourselves. We are naturally wary, willing to wait and see how the other person responds to our tiniest of gestures. We give ourselves partially. Church leaders, meanwhile, preach endlessly about commitment and loyalty—there is a disconnect between the two groups. When a person is not taught how to love themselves, they can't experience the freedom that stability brings.

When I still lived in England, the role of our leadership team at my church in Southampton was to help every one of our people to become the fullest expression of Christ that they could become. We want to set people free to be who they are in God, to serve Him as fully as they want to. I don't expect, as a leader, to be in control of that process; I expect to be a facilitator.

People have so many reasons for not letting God be God in their lives. Their excuses for soulish behavior never cease: "I've been burned before," some people say. "Once bitten, twice shy." That kind of thought actually shuts out the one Person who can heal you: God.

> "I SOMETIMES HAVE A BRIGHT DREAM OF REUNION ENGULFING US UNAWARES, LIKE A GREAT WAVE FROM BEHIND OUR BACKS — PERHAPS AT THE VERY MOMENT WHEN OUR OFFICIAL REPRESENTATIVES ARE STILL PRONOUNCING IT IMPOSSIBLE. DISCUSSIONS USUALLY SEPARATE US; ACTIONS SOMETIMES UNITE US."
> - C.S. LEWIS

God wants to come in and touch our true selves, removing all barriers and shame. He wants to flow through us, intentionally doing us good. He will overwhelm every hurdle we put up to protect ourselves from people and situations. Through His love for us, He will heal our fear of being wounded by others. When our spirit rules our soul, our attitude towards others shifts. "I know I can give you something," becomes our motto. We begin to love everybody, even blessing our own enemies, as Jesus preached in Matthew 5:44–45:

> *"But I say to you, love your enemies, bless those who curse you, do good to those who hate you, and pray for those who spitefully use you and persecute you, that you may be sons of your Father in heaven."*

GRACE AND MERCY

A spiritual Christian passes to others the kindness and mercy of God. There is more kindness of God over our lives than we'll ever be able to use. Even if we are wildly extravagant, there's more kindness available. We are swimming in His love for us! God overwhelms His children with His grace. With this kindness available, we are able to forget past issues. There is no condemnation in Christ, only a Friend who is there to help us process things and move on. God wants to love the true you and see it emerge. He speaks to the treasure in us.

His grace and mercy woos our heart. God gave us the fruit of the Spirit so we can have the fun of being like Him. Love, joy, peace, long-suffering, kindness, goodness, faithfulness, gentleness, self-control: this is how He lives His life and how He wants us to live ours. All of these gifts emerge from the inner man to be spread through the soul towards as many people as possible.

The only cure for a closed heart is a revelation of the real love of God. Nothing but His unconditional love can reach anyone. We always know where we stand with God because He never changes. His feelings for

> "THE ONLY CURE FOR A CLOSED HEART IS A REVELATION OF THE REAL LOVE OF GOD."

us never waver. We always have a place in His affections; we are always welcome in His home. The confidence that comes with His love is part of our inheritance—we must accept it. God doesn't speak to our flesh because He killed that at Calvary. He speaks to the Jesus in us because that's the value Jesus gives us before the Father. His sacrifice has made a way for us to come into God's presence at any time. He has all the power in the world, and He loves us: this would make anyone confident.

SOUL POWER
AND SOULISH NATURE

‖‖‖

The soul touched by God loves Him! It is drawn to Him but wants the relationship on its own terms: the soul wants to be in charge. This has to be broken through a process of submission and surrender. This is the work of the Cross.

There is a form of surrender which is soulish, not spiritual. We become religious when we manage our spirituality. With religiosity comes control, and with control comes the desire to dominate. This leads to others being condemned and judged if they don't see things our way.

How much of our "spirituality" is threatened by opposition? Do we feel the urge to control or dominate in human confrontations? How much of our peace is destroyed by conflict? How easily upset are we? How long does it take us to regain normal, good humor? How vulnerable are we to anger, resentment, and bitterness? How long do we hold a grudge? How quick are we to forgive? How willing are we to be restored?

If the answer to any of those questions is, in any way, negative, we are more likely living in our soul than our spirit.

God is breaking our controlling self by enabling us to submit to the spiritual fruit of self-control. Our dominating, manipulative self must become humble and submissive to Christ. We must learn to reassert our will as the vehicle of the spirit over our emotions and thought life.

We are learning to renew our minds in the spirit, so we might think as God thinks about people and situations. The soul is governed by the mind of Christ. We learn to develop faith to rule our feelings so we are not always fluctuating between doubt and trust. We learn to kill our pharisaical religiosity through the joyful imposition of unconditional love.

CONVERTED MAN

Earlier, we looked at what an unregenerate man looks like; now, I would like to give a picture of the converted man. Conversion brings us into the presence of God; the whole point of church is to maintain that presence and teach people how to abide in it. *"If you abide in Me, and My words abide in you, you will ask what you desire, and it shall be done for you,"* Jesus said in John 15:7. Whatever we want, He will do, if we are abiding in Him: now, that's power!

Jesus, according to 1 Corinthians 15, is a life-giving spirit sent to regenerate our spiritual beings. The new birth He told Nicodemus about in John 3 means that man's spirit can be recreated and restored to a living relationship with God. When that salvation occurs, the spirit must be restored to its place of primacy over the soul. When the soul gives up its power to rule and the human spirit is filled with the Holy Spirit, the power of God is released to sanctify and bring harmony to all of the faculties of the soul.

This harmony can be called "wholeness." Scripture speaks of wholeness in several places. When we read that a person was made whole, we interpret that to mean a physical healing. But God is more concerned with wholeness than with healing. Healing is just a part of being made whole. When Jesus prayed for people and they were made whole, they didn't just get healed of their ailment—their entire being was made whole.

"I THINK IT MUST HURT THE TENDER LOVE OF OUR FATHER WHEN WE PRESS FOR REASONS FOR HIS DEALINGS WITH US, AS THOUGH HE WERE NOT LOVE, AS THOUGH NOT HE BUT ANOTHER CHOSE OUR INHERITANCE FOR US, AND AS THOUGH WHAT HE CHOSE TO ALLOW COULD BE LESS THAN THE VERY BEST AND DEAREST THAT LOVE ETERNAL HAD TO GIVE."
-AMY CARMICHAEL

To be saved, the soul must come to the cross, not to be destroyed, but to give up its right to rule. Only then can it be liberated. Salvation, then, is a process; we have been saved, we are being saved, we will be saved. We need to constantly examine our lives and see what part of it needs to go before the cross, be saved, and be brought under the rule of God. It is one thing to make Jesus our Savior, and a completely different thing to make Him our Lord.

The soul does not fully comprehend the ways of God. It has no wisdom, only knowledge. That knowledge is forged by previous experience, and can plateau at a certain level and remain there for years. The spirit, however, can interact with God's wisdom through revelation. Revelation unfolds the mysteries of God as we progress in our spiritual journey. The soul is subject to that revelation and mystery, but cannot perceive either; only the spirit can. Submission increases our vision and capacity to see in the realm of the spirit.

Our spirit is intended to give us access to divine wisdom, which allows us to direct our life according to the will of God. Humanity was never intended to have independent resources of wisdom to operate our own lives through. We are brilliantly clever, but a lot of that cleverness leads to destruction. We need God's wisdom to keep that cleverness from being dangerous. Our clever brilliance has led us, for example, to rape the planet, using up its resources and polluting it at an astonishing and sickening rate. Man is a genius, but without the wisdom of God, we act insanely.

Wisdom is the ability to choose right goals and achieve them through godly means. God gives us that wisdom, and it can be found in our spirit. Knowledge lives in our head, but the wisdom of God flows from our spirit. Our level of wisdom, therefore, is not dependent on intelligence, education, common

> **"WHAT IS 'SPIRIT'? SPIRIT IS: TO LIVE AS THOUGH DEAD [DEAD TO THE WORLD]."**
> **– SOREN KIERKEGAARD**

sense, experience, culture or age. These are all valid forms of knowledge, but they are not the wisdom that comes from God.

Because of this access to divine wisdom, God ordained that the human spirit be the part of our being which directs us. God's order is clear: the Holy Spirit rules our spirit, our spirit rules our mind, and our mind rules our body. Adam was given dominion over all of creation based on this divine order. In the Garden of Eden, he and Eve were perfectly whole with no opening for sin or sickness to creep in. The enemy, in his deviousness, subverted Adam's spirit to come under his soulish desires. He wrecked God's perfect order.

A spiritual man uses his soul as a vehicle for his spirit. He takes what is happening internally—what God is revealing to you—and uses the soul to reveal it outwardly. The soul was meant as a link between body and spirit. It is designed to fulfill our destiny of introducing the wisdom and values of the spiritual realm to the natural world.

Spirit life knows where the source of wholeness is: God. When we live in our souls, we're always sitting around, waiting for something to happen. We're like the man who laid by the pool of Bethesda for years, waiting thirty-eight years for an angel to stir the water so he could be healed. Jesus arrived on the scene and asked him if he wanted to get well. Sometimes, we don't want to be healed; we'd rather wear our pain like a cloak.

> "NOT ONLY DO WE NOT KNOW GOD EXCEPT THROUGH JESUS CHRIST; WE DO NOT EVEN KNOW OURSELVES EXCEPT THROUGH JESUS CHRIST."
> - BLAISE PASCAL

A soulish man sits and waits for something to happen but a spiritual man knows that God is always working. "No need to wait," a spirit-led Christian says, "I just need to find out what

God wants to do today and get in on it." We are our own revival when we live the way God wants us to live.

ADOPTED BY GOD

As the Holy Spirit intermingles with our spirit, a quickening takes place. In this moment, a divine acceleration can occur. As our soul dies to itself, our spirit's life flourishes. People who are led by the spirit are true representatives of God. They are the very sons and daughters of God, the *huios* of God, as the Greek language puts it.

God wants to put us into a place of sonship, a deep relationship with Him where power and authority can flow. He longs to adopt us, but not in the way we use the word in the modern, western world. It is not about taking someone who is not your child and bringing them into your family; we are all born again of the spirit and are already children of the Father. God doesn't want legally-bought children, He wants love-bought children. Adoption, in ancient Hebrew times, was a ceremony that marked a rite of passage for a son, where his male parent went from being "Daddy" to a more mature "Father." Adoption is about moving from childlike immaturity to a more compelling, fuller relationship with God as the Lord of our life. He wants to make us into His *huios*.

The adoption ceremony always involved the community. A son would grow up in his daddy's house, taking on more responsibility as he got older, learning to be trustworthy and faithful. Daddy would correct him here and there, and eventually the child would come to the place where he could be trusted. At that moment, the father would call for a ceremony of adoption in the village square and put on a big feast. In the midst of the party, dad would stand up and call his son forward. In front of the whole community, he would say, "This is my son, in whom I am well pleased." At that moment, the son became like the father. If he wrote a check, the dad would honor it. If the boy gave his word, it was as if the father had himself. A son's promise committed the father. The boy could act and speak for the father. He was the father's fully-mature son, his *huios*. The community's demeanor toward the child shifted after the feast. They would treat the son the same as they treated the father from that moment on.

I would love to see this ceremony of adoption come back into the church as a rite of passage. Imagine a generation of men and women being mentored and then released at the same level as their mentor. What do we have now in the church? Membership. A person's name is put on a roll; they are given a tithe number. It's heartbreaking.

"THE SON OF GOD IS THE TEACHER OF MEN, GIVING TO THEM OF HIS SPIRIT — THAT SPIRIT WHICH MANIFESTS THE DEEP THINGS OF GOD, BEING TO A MAN THE MIND OF CHRIST."
-GEORGE MACDONALD

An adoption ceremony would be so much fuller.

Bringing an equipped, loved, and proven person forward and releasing them in front of the entire church community is so much richer than a membership card. We should be releasing our sons as *huios*, laying hands on them, and recognizing their ministries. Adoption was a communal recognition of a relational truth. This is what should happen when we set out elders or deacons. The person should be recognized, respected and released to lead.

The spirit of adoption enables our relationship with God to change from *abba* (Greek for Daddy) to *pater* (Greek for Father). We move from immaturity to maturity, as God leads us through the process. We move away from being children toward being His sons. To do this takes the breaking of our soulish nature; we must live our lives in the spirit, proving ourselves to the Father.

When we commission people for ministry, we are doing the same thing: recognizing their gift, growth, maturity, and integrity. The real anointing of God is only bestowed in sonship because it is a relational thing. In Southampton, we wouldn't dream of releasing someone into ministry if there wasn't a relational connection because we don't want to see people as functions. We want to know them, to see them grow, to see

"THIS IS MY SON, IN WHOM I AM WELL PLEASED."

them mature into their fullest expression of God. Then we can release them before the whole church, and their anointing will be recognized by our community.

CONCLUSION

To live in the glory of God, we must walk the pathway of submitting our soul to our spirit. We must take our thoughts captive, and control our emotions. Our will must move to center stage, deciding to submit to the power of our spirit. If our emotions are dominant, we won't feel like doing this. If our intellect controls us, we'll think up a way to get out of it. The will must take command of the soul. *"Work out your own salvation with fear and trembling; for it is God who works in you both to will and to do for His good pleasure,"* Paul wrote in Philippians 2:12–13.

God wants to activate our will so it can dominate our thinking and our feeling. Our will pushes the soul under the spirit, allowing God to shine through and do what He wants to do. Exercising the will is a cold-blooded act. "I will do this thing. No matter what I feel, I'll do it."

As we use our will to force our soul to submit, it becomes easier and easier to do. Our faith in God grows as we see what He is doing all around us. As David sang in Psalm 27:13: *"I would have lost heart, unless I had believed that I would see the goodness of the Lord in the land of the living."* Our will allows us to see how big God can be, and helps us to trust that the Holy Spirit will make us more like Jesus.

When the soul comes under the rule of the spirit, life and peace are the result. Suddenly, we don't have to know everything; we just become wise about where to stand at any given moment. We don't know how everything will pan out, but we learn to be happy with the process of getting there. We become fixated on holding God's hand, and not worried about the trouble around us.

God does, at times, lift our eyes up to the horizon and reveal where we are going. But when He doesn't, a spiritual man or woman should still be content, happy to walk out His journey step by step. This walk of faith is brilliant. Sometimes, God keeps us from seeing what's down the road because He is jealous for our love. He wants us to be fully preoccupied with Him. Other times, He opens the windows and you can see into the future. God will always give you the right amount of light; whether it be for the next step of your journey or the next one hundred miles.

God has so much more for us than the soulish lives we have lived. His Spirit longs to mingle with our own, giving us the wisdom, revelation, assurance, and love that will develop us into amazing spiritual beings. The first step is to use our will to choose to come under our spirit's rule. This is the beginning of His dream for us.

JESUS IS LORD

Beloved. You resist the enemy not by fighting his mind forays but by submitting to the mind of Christ within. Learn to turn and yield your thoughts to Mine. Practice will enable you to take thoughts captive.

The place of deliverance is within you. It is the safe and holy place of the inner man of your spirit, where My life rules and reigns supreme. In this delightful discipline, I will create a fortress in your mind as you cooperate with Me.

There is an equalizing pressure within that not only disregards enemy attacks on the mind but also delivers a positive truth and perspective to counter enemy assaults on your life and others around you.

In this next season, the battle for your mind and thought life will intensify because this is the time of your appointed breakthrough.

I am going to enable you to enjoy peace of mind. As you give away your worries, anxieties, and fears, you will experience an eternal victory that is being shaped and influenced by holy thinking.

CHART 1

WHAT IS THE SOUL?	WHAT IS THE SPIRIT?
MIND	SHARES THE MIND OF CHRIST
WILL	SURRENDERS TO THE CROSS
EMOTIONS	COMES UNDER TRUST AND FAITH
THE OUTER MAN	THE INNER MAN
THE OUTER BEING	THE INNER BEING
A VEHICLE FOR THE SPIRIT	A VEHICLE FOR THE HOLY SPIRIT
FRUIT FROM THE TREE OF THE KNOWLEDGE OF GOOD AND EVIL	FRUIT FROM THE TREE OF LIFE
CONTROLS THE BODY	CONTROLS THE SOUL
WANTS SELF-GRATIFICATION	SUBJECT TO GOD
MARTHA (LUKE 10:38-42)	MARY (10:38-42)
CAIN (GENESIS 4)	ABEL (GENESIS 4)
CARNAL	SPIRITUAL
CAN LIVE IN RELIGIOSITY	CAN ONLY LIVE BY THE HOLY SPIRIT
PREOCCUPIED WITH THE FIRST HEAVEN	PREOCCUPIED WITH THE THIRD HEAVEN
ALWAYS SEEKING REASSURANCE	KNOWS ITS HOME IN THE LOVE OF GOD
PERFORMANCE CHRISTIANITY	PASSIONATE CHRISTIANITY
WANTS STATUS, POSITION, FAME	SEEKS HUMILITY, REST, AND OBSCURITY

CHART 2

WHAT IS THE FIRST HEAVEN?	THE EARTH; THE PHYSICAL REALM; WHERE OUR SOUL AND BODY OPERATE
WHAT IS THE SECOND HEAVEN?	WHERE SATAN AND HIS DEMONIC FORCES OPERATE; THE KINGDOM OF EVIL AND DARKNESS
WHAT IS THE THIRD HEAVEN?	WHERE GOD'S THRONE ROOM RESIDES; ACCESSIBLE BY OUR SPIRIT INTERMINGLING WITH THE HOLY SPIRIT; THE KINGDOM OF GOD AND LIGHT

MEDITATION

A MEETING: IN THE SECRET PLACE

Come and join me,
I'm drawing you into a quiet place
Of introspection.
Come away from the noise,
Into the place of stillness.

No, beloved, I'm not talking of externals,
I'm not speaking of a physical place that you need to reach.

There is a safe place within you,
A quiet place, where stillness reigns.
I'm asking you to retreat from the soul—
Your Martha of many distractions—
Legitimate, powerful, necessary,
but ultimately unhelpful
— compared to what I want to give you.

Step back into your spirit
Through the inner fortress of your heart,
Away from the world and the busyness of your soul.

Meet the Mary that it is your spirit man
And come to sit at My feet.

I'm here, in the secret place of our spirit,
Waiting.
All you need is here by Me.

Provision, peace and a rest for your soul—
Come and sit quietly by Me.

I am the pool of water by your feet
I am the manna falling
I am the raven feeding you
The tree of life that gives you shade
I am the gentle breeze that kisses your brow
I am the eagle's cry, watching over you from above
I am the velvet paws of the lion, padding protectively
around your camp.

Step back, far back into your spirit,
Practice being still, learn the way of peace.

I will deal with the issues,
Remove the spots and blemishes,
Refine your heart.

I will empty you of all that you
don't need and never wanted,
I will purge and purify your heart.

I will imprison Eros and release Agape within you.
All self-obsession, ambition, preservation
Will die in you
I will empty you of all that grieves Me and frustrates you
And fill the vacuum with worship.

Out of that place of eternal rest
Will come a new creation
Soft, pliable
Owning nothing yet possessing all things.

A servant will merge with the son.
A warrior will grow out of the child.
Action will flow out of rest
In the secret place of your spirit.

The enemy cannot find you.
The vagaries of life leave you untouched
Impurities will be drawn away from your heart
In the quiet strength of My presence.

The aching, the longing in your heart
Will be overshadowed by all My desire for you.
You shall be fully known
And you will know.

A MEDITATION
ON RESTING
IN GOD

What you have to focus on now is the incomparable love of God for you. Right now, where you are, He adores you. He couldn't love you any more than He loves you at this very moment. This is the thing that He wants to plant in your heart: "I love you, I've always loved you, and I always will love you. I love you one hundred percent, right now. Be at peace."

There is no good time to learn about resting: there just isn't. There will always be something that will prevent you from resting. Psalm 46 opens with an earthquake and ends with *"Be still, and know that I am God."* Mark 4 has a storm threatening the safety and security of the disciples. The antidote was to speak peace, as Jesus did. But if you can rest now, you can rest at any other time. God has given you permission to rest when you are in turmoil about yourself. What are you resting in? You're resting in the fact that God adores you, right now. You're resting in His ability to change you all the time. And you're resting in the fact that you are totally acceptable to Him. It doesn't matter what is occurring around or within you. You are acceptable in Christ. So rest.

Study Matthew 11:28–30:

Come to Me, all you who labor and are heavy laden, and I will give you rest. Take My yoke upon you and learn from Me, for I am gentle and lowly in heart, and you will find rest for your souls. For My yoke is easy and My burden is light.

A yoke is a harness which fits over the shoulders. It connects us to the one walking alongside and enables us to move in unison. Jesus has promised us that if we walk with Him we can bear our burdens in a completely different manner. What would the freedom to rest really bring us in our busy lives?

Let the Father's peace fall in your life, a peace that transcends all understanding. Ask the Lord to come and wash your mind in His peace. Let it fall on you. Pray that the Prince of Peace would come to you. Ask Him to take away worry, fear, doubt, self-loathing, self-hatred, your masks, and your pretenses, leaving only peace in their place. He first loved us, and with Him, we will win this battle of spirit over soul. It's going to be a good fight, but your spirit is going to win.

Identify your current unrest or lack of peace. What are you not seeing about God's power or faithfulness? Does your lack of peace arise out of a wrong perception? What needs to change so that peace may remain? Sometimes peace is restored by the simple act of pushing away worry, fear, anxiety, panic, and unbelief. Try it. Get tough on the causes of unrest within yourself. The writer of Hebrews calls it laboring to enter that rest (Hebrews 4:8–11). We have to work at being at peace!

DEALING
WITH
DISILLUSIONMENT

It is impossible for God to become disillusioned with us; He never had any illusions about us in the first place. The Lord knows exactly who each of us is. On the day we came to Him, we couldn't have been in a worse state. He saw us at absolute rock bottom. And still, He pursued us, found us, and kissed us. He loved us one hundred percent then, and still does now. We have no reason to hide from His love.

When we live in our soul, we always look for reassurance. Our grip on our relationship with God is always shaky; we feel like we don't really belong to Him. But the problem isn't that God has illusions about us—it's that we have illusions about Him!

We often ascribe human qualities to God, rather than divine ones. "God must be really annoyed with me," we think. "How could He ever forgive me?"

Years ago, I came to the Lord and said, "I'm sorry, I keep coming back to You with the same issue."

"What issue?" He replied. "This is the first time you've come to Me with this."

"No, I did it yesterday, Lord."

"Oh, I forgot all about that," He said. "That was yesterday and it's under the blood of Christ—it no longer speaks of failure."

My daughter Sophie says God has a memory like a thousand elephants, except when it comes to sin. If we have repented, our sin is under the blood and He has forgotten all about it. Our souls can't accept that sometimes, because we are subject to doubt, fear, insecurity, and unbelief. We become disillusioned with each other.

I once had a man come to me and tell me that he was disillusioned with me.

"Thank God for that!" I said. "Disillusionment is the breaking of your illusions. You had illusions about me, and now they're broken. That means we can have a real relationship based on truth, not illusion. We can enter into reality together."

I have friends that know what I'm like on a good day, and know what I'm like on a bad day. They know the areas where I'm tempted to sin. They know it all because they ask me very awkward questions. But we have given each other that right. My life is incredibly safe because of the fact that I have people who love me whether I am doing well, or poorly. This is real friendship.

Disillusionment is a stage we go through in order to get real. It brings us to deeper communion and friendship. It rips away our veneers of respectability. We all wear masks and hide behind an image of ourselves; real friendship gets behind that mask. We must get disillusioned with one another and move on into reality. Kleenex relationships, where we use one another and throw each other away, are ruining the church. When we meet a man or woman who is ruled by the spirit, there is a humility that reaches out and touches us. Their brokenness will move us. Their gentleness, meekness, peace will touch us powerfully. We feel at ease with that person, and able to share ourselves. The masks slip away.

With soulish people, the mask stays firmly in place. Instinctively, we know that if they see behind the mask, they'll kill us spiritually. Bondages cannot be broken in soulish ministry. Our belief systems cannot be truly changed by soul power. We will live in the illusions we have about ourselves and others.

QUESTIONS FOR MEDITATION

✦ REGARDING PAST RELATIONSHIPS THAT DID NOT WORK OUT: HAVE YOU EVER EXPERIENCED DISILLUSIONMENT OVER SOMEONE?

- WHAT ILLUSIONS DID YOU HAVE THAT WERE BROKEN?

- DID YOU LET GO OF THE RELATIONSHIP BECAUSE OF THIS?

- IN WHAT WAY COULD YOU HAVE SEEN THEM AND THE SITUATION DIFFERENTLY?

- WHAT WOULD NEED TO CHANGE IN YOU IN ORDER FOR YOU TO SEE THEM AS GOD DOES?

- IF DISILLUSIONMENT IS A DOORWAY INTO A DEEPER REALITY, WHAT FRUIT(S) OF THE SPIRIT MUST BE ESTABLISHED IN YOU SO THAT YOUR ENHANCED VISION CAN CREATE A DEEPER PLACE OF UNDERSTANDING/EMPATHY TO IMPROVE YOUR RELATIONSHIPS?

- HOW WILL YOU ENABLE THIS TO HAPPEN THROUGH YOUR COOPERATION WITH THE HOLY SPIRIT?

✦ ARE YOU DISILLUSIONED WITH GOD?

_____

_____

_____

   – WHAT IS IT ABOUT YOUR CURRENT PERCEPTION OF
     GOD THAT IS NOT WORKING FOR YOU?

_____

_____

_____

   – WHAT IS THE PLACE WITHIN THAT THE HOLY SPIRIT
     IS SEEKING TO BUILD SO THAT A GREATER SENSE OF
     HIS PRESENCE CAN BE FOUND?

_____

_____

_____

   – WHAT IS THE CURRENT CONFLICT WITHIN YOU
     THAT REQUIRES A DEEPER PEACE AND A GREATER
     REVELATION OF TRUTH?

_____

_____

_____

– WHAT IS THE FATHER'S VISION OF YOU THAT FORMS PART OF THE "TRUTH THAT SETS YOU FREE"?

– IF REPENTANCE IS ABOUT CHANGING YOUR MINDSET, WHAT OLD THINKING MUST YOU DELETE FROM YOUR MIND AND WHAT NEW THOUGHTS MUST BE ESTABLISHED THROUGH EVERY DAY EXPERIENCE?

– IF REVELATION IS A SPRINGBOARD TO EXPERIENCE, WHAT NEW EXPECTATIONS OF GOD IS THE HOLY SPIRIT DEVELOPING IN YOUR LIFE?

– HOW WILL THIS NEW EXPERIENCE/EXPECTATION AFFECT YOUR LIFESTYLE OF FAITH AND YOUR THINKING ABOUT THE FUTURE?

✦ REGARDING CURRENT RELATIONSHIPS THAT ARE HARD: EXPLAIN HOW YOU WILL LOOK AT CURRENT FRIENDSHIPS AND THE POSSIBILITY OF NEW RELATIONSHIPS FROM A MORE SPIRITUAL PERSPECTIVE.

- WHO CAN YOU BE "REAL" WITH? NAME PEOPLE.

- HOW CAN YOU SEE BEYOND THE MASK THEY WEAR? HOW CAN YOU APPRECIATE AND VALUE THEM AS PEOPLE STRUGGLING TO CONFORM TO JESUS?

- HOW CAN YOU LET YOUR OWN MASK DROP AND DEVELOP A MORE TRUSTING RELATIONSHIP WITH YOUR CURRENT FRIENDS?

✦ WHAT IS UNCONDITIONAL, NON-NEGOTIABLE LOVE LIKE, IN YOUR VIEW?

- HOW CAN YOU EXPERIENCE IT IN CHRIST?

- HOW CAN YOU MINISTER IT TO OTHERS?

- WHAT IS YOUR OWN INTERNAL PLACE OF SAFETY IN CHRIST (YOUR REFUGE/HIGH TOWER) FROM WHICH YOU CAN EXPERIENCE AND BE CHANGED BY SUCH LOVE?

- HOW DO YOU PLAN TO LOCATE AND USE SUCH LOVE ON BEHALF OF OTHER PEOPLE?

PERFORMANCE
CHRISTIANITY

Where there is no self-love, our love for others is limited and often conditional. This is the heart of what I call Performance Christianity. Many Christians live with a sense of unworthiness. Our true self is still imprisoned; a slave to do things that will win us acceptance or approval. We haven't let ourselves out of the jail Jesus came to free us from.

When Jesus came out of the wilderness after forty days, He immediately began to speak about His ministry. Before that test, He had been with the people, sharing about God. After the test, He went to the church of the day to announce His ministry. He went immediately to a company of people who thought they belonged to God. When he got there, He took Scripture out of sequence and read Isaiah 61:1:

> *"The Spirit of the Lord GOD is upon Me,*
> *Because the LORD has anointed Me*
> *To preach good tidings to the poor;*
> *He has sent Me to heal the brokenhearted,*
> *To proclaim liberty to the captives,*
> *And the opening of the prison to those who are bound."*

The prisoner He came to free was the Church of His day.

Sometimes I think there are more people bound inside of the Church than there are outside of it. Bound by pharisaical behavior, by religiosity, by a system that doesn't set them free to be who they are in God. We have become conformed, not to God, but to the religious system of our day. We find lots of teachers telling us what to do, but very few fathers, releasing us to learn how to become sons. And we wonder why people leave the Church in droves!

I love the Church, with all of her flaws, idiosyncrasies, and weirdness. There is no plan B for God—the Church is all we have. We have to find a way to become a company of people that gladden the heart of God together and are intensely supernatural in the Earth.

"The opening of the prison to those who are bound": Jesus spoke those words to the church of His day, and He speaks them to us again. To win this battle against Performance Christianity, we must learn to love ourselves, and to love God and our neighbors as fully as that. The problem is that we already love our neighbors as we love ourselves: we don't like ourselves, and we have little patience for other people.

Performance Christians pray and give to be seen. Everything is about appearance and being noticed. The soul is not broken in these people. Our soul wants recognition in the form of status, position, titles, and fame. The spirit is just content to live in the presence of God. We must get into our spirit.

"For those who live according to the flesh set their minds on the things of the flesh, but those who live according to the Spirit, the things of the Spirit. For to be carnally minded is death, but to be spiritually minded is life and peace," Paul wrote in Romans 8:5–6. Those who live in their soul can please God periodically, but not continually. The spirit man, however, can dwell in Him, and He in the spirit man. We must have that Spirit of Christ.

People who live in the soul seldom have clear victories. There is always something left undone; no real ground is taken.

They battle over the same issue again and again and again. Performance Christians have no progression in their lives. They are up and down over everything.

A performance mentality seeks to earn a relationship with God through activity. Scripture talks about faith and works (in that order). Our faith is justified when we act on what we believe about God and ourselves. God's love enables. God's power releases. His life within develops our lifestyle without. He is the Creator, the Architect, the Builder. All flows from Him. His life moves from the inside to the outside of our life.

Our relationship *with* God is the motivating factor. We love others in the way that we are loved by the Lord. We serve the Lord out of gratitude for all that He is, and all that He has done in our lives. We are not trying to get anywhere with God, we recognize that, in Christ, we are already there; and in our experience of grace are also becoming more of who we really are in Christ. It's a wonderful paradox that sets us free to be and to become.

Performance Christians live in the opposite manner, doing everything to feel accepted and acceptable to God. They think that attending meetings, praying more, witnessing, serving, and reading the Bible more will bring them closer to God. Our relationship with the Father is based on what Christ has accomplished on the Cross. We are accepted in the beloved (Ephesians 1). There is nothing we can do to earn God's love and we cannot be condemned. Grace and mercy are poured out upon us constantly as part of our salvation gift.

We have more grace and mercy than we can conceivably use for ourselves, so we can allow it to be poured through us to others. In this way, we are true representatives of the Father's heart to all people. Performance-oriented people have little patience or love for others. They see faults rather than potential. They condemn sin rather than release mercy. They speak truth without grace. They rely on self-effort rather than acceptance in Christ as the foundation for their experience. However, they rightly express that *"Faith without works is dead."* But they do not understand that works which are not dependent upon acceptance and faith of what God is doing in us can never provide what God seeks to release.

The fact is that we pray, witness, serve, read Scripture, and attend meetings not to reach out to God but to express our sheer enjoyment that He is reaching out to us. It is how we celebrate His love. He is with us, He is for us, and we wriggle with the pleasure of His joy in us. He sings over us. He laughs at our enemies. He forgives so readily. He understands us completely. In the spirit, we learn to live every day under His smile. Our soul strives for the acceptance that our spirit so readily receives.

QUESTIONS FOR MEDITATION

IIIIIIIIIIIIIIIIIIIIIIIIIIIIIIIIIIIIIIIIIIIIIIIIIIIIIIIIIIIIIIIIIIIIIIIIIIIIIIIIIIIIIIIIIIIIIIIIIIIIIIIIIIIIIIIIIIIIII

✦ DO YOU STRUGGLE WITH ACCEPTING WHO YOU ARE IN CHRIST?

_____

_____

_____

- HOW EASY DO YOU FIND IT TO TRUST IN ALL THAT THE FATHER HAS PROVIDED FOR YOU IN JESUS?

_____

_____

_____

- WHAT ARE THE MAJOR BARRIERS TO SELF-ACCEPTANCE?

_____

_____

_____

- DO YOUR EMOTIONS RUN THE SHOW IN TERMS OF YOUR SPIRITUALITY? FOR EXAMPLE, IF YOUR EMOTIONS WERE RUNNING COUNTER TO WHAT YOU SHOULD BELIEVE, WHICH WOULD DOMINATE?

_____

_____

_____

- WHAT IS THE EFFECT OF YOUR NON-ACCEPTANCE
  IN CHRIST ON YOUR OTHER RELATIONSHIPS?

- DO YOU FEEL YOU NEED TO DO ANYTHING TO EARN
  GOD'S LOVE OR APPROVAL?

- WHAT IS PREVENTING YOU FROM LIVING AS A
  MUCH-LOVED CHILD BEFORE THE FATHER?

EXTRA EXERCISE: LECTIO DIVINA

Lectio Divina (Latin for *divine reading*) is an ancient way of reading the Bible—allowing a quiet and contemplative way of coming to God's Word. Lectio Divina opens the pulse of the Scripture, helping readers dig far deeper into the Word than normally happens in a quick glance-over.

In this exercise, we will look at a portion of Scripture and use a modified Lectio Divina technique to engage it. This technique can be used on any piece of Scripture; I highly recommend using it for key Bible passages that the Lord has highlighted for you, and for anything you think might be an inheritance word for your life (see the Crafted Prayer interactive journal for more on inheritance words).

Romans 8:

There is therefore now no condemnation to those who are in Christ Jesus, who do not walk according to the flesh, but according to the Spirit. For the law of the Spirit of life in Christ Jesus has made me free from the law of sin and death. For what the law could not do in that it was weak through the flesh, God did by sending His own Son in the likeness of sinful flesh, on account of sin: He condemned sin in the flesh, that the righteous requirement of the law might be fulfilled in us who do not walk according to the flesh but according to the Spirit. For those who live according to the flesh set their minds on the things of the flesh, but those who live according to the Spirit, the things of the Spirit. For to be carnally minded is death, but to be spiritually minded is life and peace. Because the carnal mind is enmity against God; for it is not subject to the law of God, nor indeed can be. So then, those who are in the flesh cannot please God.

But you are not in the flesh but in the Spirit, if indeed the Spirit of God dwells in you. Now if anyone does not have the Spirit of Christ, he is not His. And if Christ is in you, the body is dead because of sin, but the Spirit is life because of righteousness. But if the Spirit of Him who raised Jesus from the dead dwells in you, He who raised Christ from the dead will also give life to your mortal bodies through His Spirit who dwells in you.

Therefore, brethren, we are debtors—not to the flesh, to live according to the flesh. For if you live according to the flesh you will die; but if by the Spirit you put to death the deeds of the body, you will live. For as many as are led by the Spirit of God, these are sons of God. For you did not receive the spirit of bondage again to fear, but you received the Spirit of adoption by whom we cry out, "Abba, Father." The Spirit Himself bears witness with our spirit that we are children of God, and if children, then heirs—heirs of God and joint heirs with Christ, if indeed we suffer with Him, that we may also be glorified together.

For I consider that the sufferings of this present time are not worthy to be compared with the glory which shall be revealed in us. For the earnest expectation of the creation eagerly waits for the revealing of the sons of God. For the creation was subjected to futility, not willingly, but because of Him

- FOLLOWING THE READING, MEDITATE UPON WHAT YOU HAVE HEARD. WHAT STANDS OUT? WRITE IT DOWN:

_____

_____

_____

- IF A WORD OR PHRASE FROM THE PASSAGE SEEMS HIGHLIGHTED TO YOU, WRITE IT DOWN:

_____

_____

_____

✦ READ THE PASSAGE TWICE, AGAIN.

- LIKE WAVES CRASHING ONTO A SHORE, LET THE WORDS OF THE SCRIPTURE CRASH ONTO YOUR SPIRIT. WHAT ARE YOU DISCERNING? WHAT ARE YOU HEARING? WHAT ARE YOU FEELING? WRITE IT DOWN:

_____

_____

_____

- WHAT IS THE THEME OF THIS PASSAGE? WRITE IT DOWN:

_____

_____

_____

- DOES THIS PASSAGE REKINDLE ANY MEMORIES OR EXPERIENCES? WRITE IT DOWN:

_____

_____

- WHAT IS THE HOLY SPIRIT SAYING TO YOU? WRITE IT DOWN:

✦ READ THE PASSAGE TWO FINAL TIMES.
  - MEDITATE ON IT.
  - IS THERE SOMETHING GOD WANTS YOU TO DO WITH THIS PASSAGE? IS THERE SOMETHING HE IS CALLING YOU TO? WRITE IT DOWN:

  - PRAY SILENTLY. TELL GOD WHAT THIS SCRIPTURE IS LEADING YOU TO THINK ABOUT. ASK HIM FOR HIS THOUGHTS. WRITE DOWN YOUR CONVERSATION—AS IF YOU AND GOD ARE SITTING IN A COFFEE SHOP, TWO OLD AND DEAR FRIENDS, SHARING:

✦ PRAY AND THANK GOD FOR WHAT HE HAS SHARED WITH YOU. COME BACK TO THE PASSAGE A FEW MORE TIMES OVER THE COMING WEEKS.

ABOUT THE AUTHOR

Graham and Theresa Cooke reside in Santa Barbara, California. Working together with their closest friends they have formed a Kingdom community called Radiance. Radiance is a community of creatives and entrepreneurs with a citywide focus on Arts and Business. While individual members of the community are involved in a wide range of Kingdom activities (i.e. caring for the poor, teaching/training, pastoral ministry) the community, as a whole, is focused on impacting the social pillars of Arts and Business in Santa Barbara. They are committed to making a place for Kingdom-minded dreamers to explore and realize the potential of their imagination—and to raising the "water level" of Kingdom Culture in this city.

He is married to Theresa who has a passion for worship and dance. She loves to be involved in intercession, warfare and setting people free. She cares about injustice, abuse and has compassion for people who are sick, suffering and disenfranchised.

Graham and Theresa have a growing family spanning two generations and several countries. All their children are involved in business, the arts and entertainment. There are numerous grandchildren who keep them busy laughing and enjoying life.

Graham is a popular conference speaker and is well known for his training programs on the prophetic, spiritual warfare, intimacy and devotional life, leadership, spirituality and the church in transition. He functions as a consultant and freethinker to businesses, churches and organizations, enabling them to develop strategically. He has a passion to establish the Kingdom and build prototype churches that can fully reach a post-modern society.

A strong part of Graham's ministry is in producing finances and resources for the poor and disenfranchised in developing countries. He supports many projects specifically for widows, orphans and people in the penal system. He hates the abuse of women and works actively against human trafficking and the sex slave trade; including women caught up in prostitution and pornography.

Graham is an ambassador for communities of faith in the Body of Christ on behalf of Not For Sale. He talks about the work of Not For Sale and empowers individuals, families, businesses, ministries and churches to get involved in sponsoring projects. Not For Sale have specific assignments that involve rescue, restoration and providing education; skills-based training and small business development to enable people to become fully rehabilitated into a normal, productive life.

If you would like to invite Graham to minister at an event, please complete our online Ministry Invitation Form at BrilliantPersepctives.com.

If you want to give to Not For Sale and partner with them directly, it's simple. Go to their website, NotForSaleCampaign.org.

Look at the range of what they are doing and at the very least give a one time gift, or give a monthly donation for six months or one year. Better still; involve your family, friends, business or church in sponsoring a specific project.

Your contribution makes a world of difference to the people rescued by your involvement.

FAQs

Q: WHO IS GRAHAM COOKE AND HOW CAN I FIND MORE INFORMATION ON HIM?

A: GRAHAM IS A SPEAKER, AUTHOR AND MENTOR WHO LIVES IN SANTA BARBARA, CALIFORNIA. HE IS PART OF A CHRISTIAN COMMUNITY CALLED RADIANCE THAT HAS A PASSION FOR BUSINESS AND THE ARTS.

YOU CAN CONTACT HIM AT WWW.BRILLIANTPERSPECTIVES.COM

Q: HOW CAN I BECOME A PRAYER PARTNER WITH GRAHAM?

A: GRAHAM HAS A COMPANY OF TRAINED PROPHETIC INTERCESSORS CALLED THE WARRIOR CLASS, WHICH IS OVERSEEN BY ALLISON BOWN, WHO IS THE DIRECTOR.

TO CONTACT ALLISON PLEASE GO TO THE WARRIOR CLASS WEBSITE, WWW.TWCLASS.ORG.

Q: HAS GRAHAM WRITTEN ANY OTHER BOOKS?

A: FOR A FULL AND UP TO DATE LIST OF ALL GRAHAM'S BOOKS, CD'S AND RESOURCES PLEASE GO TO WWW.BRILLIANTBOOKHOUSE.COM.